Simple Computer Maintence & Repair

by Wally Wang &
Scott Millard

Editing by Cynthia Collier & Gretchen Lingham
Cover illustration & inside illustrations by Lisa Mozzini
Art direction by Kay Thorogood

Every effort has been made to supply the most current
information regarding the software publishers, and products
discussed in this book. However, CPE assumes no
responsibility for any infringements of patents or other
rights of third parties which would result.

First Edition Copyright© 1990
Computer Publishing Enterprises
P.O. Box 23478
San Diego, CA 92123

Entire contents copyright 1989 by Computer Publishing Enterprises.
All rights reserved. No part of this publication may be reproduced
in any form or by any means, electronic or mechanical, including
photocopying, recording, or by any information storage or retrieval
system, without permission from the publisher.

0-945776-10-1

CONTENTS

INTRODUCTION

Your Computer Needs TLC

A computer is more sensitive than your basic television or stereo system. Next to your car, or family, a computer requires time for maintenance and repair. This doesn't mean that your computer will break once every three months like a car, but it does mean that things can go wrong.

To keep your computer working, you need to understand what causes problems and how you an fix them. The purpose of this book is not to turn the average person into a computer technician. Instead, it is intended to give you a few tips on preventing problemsand solving them if they occur.

Part One of this book covers basic precautions that can extend the life of your computer. Although there are so many computers on the market, the princicples remain the same: take care of your computer and it will work reliably for you.

Part Two of this book describes various steps for repairing a computer. Because of the wide variety of computer brands, the majority of the procedures apply to IBM and compatible computers.

All computers use the same basic components so the maintenance and repair techniques in this book should work with any computer. If there is something in this book that doesn't apply to your particular computer, then you must call a friend that knows all about computers, or take your system to a qualified repair center.

Knowing more about computers will help you fix the majority of computer problems yourself. If a problem appears that's too difficult for you to solve, at the very least you will be able to understand what type of work needs to be done and how much it should cost.

PART 1

MAINTENANCE
by Wally Wang

CHAPTER 1

*Simple Computer
Maintenance*

So you bought yourself a computer, or you're thinking about buying one. Congratulations! Owning a computer can be fun or frustrating, depending on what happens next.

Part of the fun of owning a computer is using it. Nothing can sap your excitement quicker than a computer that doesn't do anything but show squiggly lines on the screen.

As with cars, owning a computer demands responsibility. If you don't take care of your car, you could hurt somebody if your car skids out of control. With computers, life is a bit fairer. If you don't take care of your computer, the only person liable to suffer will be yourself.

To keep your computer in shape, you need to practice preventative maintenance. But just as you can't drive your car indefinitely without an occasional tune-up or oil change, so you need to keep your computer maintained, as well.

Keeping The Computer Happy

Preventative maintenance begins with your computer. Don't drop it, kick it, or use it as a doorstop. This is a delicate piece of electronic equipment, so treat it like a baby or something delicate inside will likely get jarred and never work again.

While you shouldn't take unnecessary risks with your computer (like take it sky-diving or wind-surfing), computers are tougher than you think. You actually *could* drop them, kick them, or use them as doorstops—they might keep working. But don't tempt fate.

Physical abuse can take less obvious forms. Keep your computer away from extreme temperature ranges. Cold temperatures may keep your computer from working, while hot temperatures can overheat the computer. Since your computer generates heat on its own, high temperatures can bake your computer's processor, memory chips, and everything else.

Think of it this way: as long as you're comfortable in the room, your computer will be comfortable, too. If sleeping in the Sahara Desert or Antarctica doesn't appeal to you, your computer won't like it, either.

The Burn-In Period

When you get a new computer, put it through a burn-in period. This means leaving the computer on for two days to two weeks straight, day and night. The burn-in period torture-tests the circuits to make sure that everything works. Either that, or it fries the living daylights out of your computer and lets you know that the computer wasn't going to work anyway.

Most computer manufacturers and dealers routinely put their computers through a 48-hour burn-in period, but you had better put yours through another burn-in period—just in case. If anything will fail, it will fail during the burn-in period. Then you can take the computer back to the dealer while its still under warranty.

Turning the Computer On and Off

Turn your computer on before you start working, and turn it off when you're done for the day; don't keep turning it on and off every time you use it.

Whenever you turn on a computer, an electric current surges through it's circuits and jolts it awake like electroshock therapy treatment. While Frankenstein might enjoy a good shock or two, your computer does not. Shock it enough times during the day and your computer just might shock you by suddenly failing and filling the room with the acrid smell of smoke.

Play it safe. Leave the computer on until you know you won't use it again for the rest of the day. The minor amount of electricity your computer uses will be a small price to pay to keep the computer working longer.

Power Surges

Power surges can come from turning your computer on and off during the day, or from your friendly neighborhood power company. To protect yourself against power surges, buy a power surge suppressor.

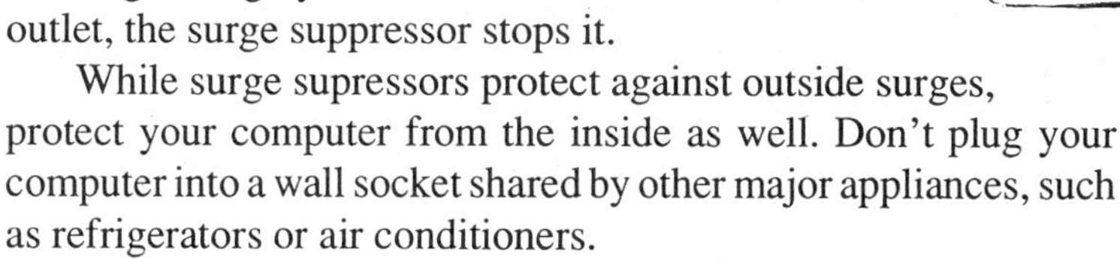

A surge suppressor does exactly what its name implies. Any time a power surge comes cruising through your electrical outlet, the surge suppressor stops it.

While surge supressors protect against outside surges, protect your computer from the inside as well. Don't plug your computer into a wall socket shared by other major appliances, such as refrigerators or air conditioners.

Whenever the other appliance turns on, it drains the electricity from anything else plugged into the same outlet. This drain only occurs for a split second, but in that time your computer may turn off, lose the data in its memory, and decide the hell with it and quit.

Storing Your Computer

Put your computer on a flat, steady surface so the computer doesn't bounce around. To save space, you can turn the computer on its side. While this doesn't hurt the computer, make sure that the computer has enough space for air to circulate.

Look in the front and back of your computer for air vents. Computers usually have fans that blow air through the case to keep the computer cool. If you block the computer's cooling vents, the computer may overheat.

As another precaution, format the hard disk after flipping the computer sideways. While not necessary, this precaution can prevent hard disk problems in the future.

Don't worry too much about your computer. Just store it in a safe place, keep it away from heat, cold, dust, water, power surges, unauthorized personnel, and over anxious children with chocolate smeared across their fingers, and your computer should be fine.

Computers usually don't fail; their parts do. The parts most likely to fail are the monitor, keyboard, and disk drives.

CHAPTER 2

Watching the Monitor

This may be confusing. Leave your computer on but shut the monitor off. If you leave the monitor on, the phosphor image "burns" into the face of the screen. So while a burn-in period can extend the life of your computer, the same burn-in period can shorten the life of your monitor.

Burn-In

When you turn on your computer, turn down (don't turn off) the monitor. If you leave the monitor turned up, the phosphor permanently etches itself into the screen. If this happens, you will need to buy another monitor.

Shock Cleaning

If you want to know what a power surge feels like to a computer, spray glass cleaner on your monitor and try to wipe it away.

Monitors generate static electricity that sucks dust to your computer screen. You can wipe this dust off with a soft cloth, but if you use a spray cleaner, watch it.

Monitors act like television sets. When you turn one off, up to 25,000 volts of electricity may still reside behind the monitor screen. The spray from a glass cleaner could (not likely, but why play odds with your life?) leak inside, sending 25,000 volts of trapped electricity surging through your body and ruining what could have been a perfectly fine day.

If you must use a liquid spray cleaner, wait an hour for the electrical charge in the monitor to subside. Then close your eyes, spray the screen, and hope that nothing happens. As a safer bet, clean your computer's monitor at the beginning of the day after the computer has been off all night. Then you can be sure that your computer won't supply you with any shocking surprises.

CHAPTER 3

Floppy and Hard Disk Drives

Computers don't like smoke. They don't like dust either, or high humidity, high temperature, or cold temperature for that matter. Come to think of it, computers don't like a whole lot.

Dust

Among all the parts of a computer, the most failure-prone are the disk drives. Disk drives read information from floppy disks like record players "read" music from a record. Just like records, floppy disks collect dust. If the computer tries to read a dusty disk, it could skip or scratch the surface, ruining your data as badly as dust might scratch a record.

To prevent this, keep your floppy disks in their protective envelopes at all times. If you use 31/2 inch floppy disks, just make sure that the metal shutter closes over the exposed part of the disk surface and your disks will be fine.

Smoke

Don't smoke around your computer. Smoke particles can settle on the floppy disk surface. When the floppy disk drive head tries to read the data on the disk, the smoke particles act like sand crystals and gouge into the surface, ruining your data.

If you don't smoke around a computer, don't start. If you do smoke, now you have an added incentive to help you break the habit (or your computer, whichever comes first).

Use Quality Floppy Disks

When you buy floppy disks, buy reliable ones. That doesn't necessarily mean buy name-brand ones. Many name-brand disk manufacturers simply buy disks from someone else and slap their name on it. The more reputable name-brand disk manufacturers make their own.

That means you can buy boxes of cheap disks and find that they all work perfectly well. Or you could buy a box of name-brand disks and find that none of them work at all. When you find disks that you trust, stick with them. A bad disk can do more than ruin your day by wiping out important data.

Remember that disks, like records, eventually wear out. Always make backup copies of your disks and store them in a separate place. That way if a disaster wipes out your computer room, it won't wipe out your original and backup disks at the same time. The time to make backup copies is now.

Hard Disks

A hard disk really *is* hard. Unlike floppy disks, a hard disk drive head never touches the disk surface, but floats over the cushion of air created when the hard disk spins. When you hear a whirring sound, that's the hard disk spinning around.

If you bumped your computer, the drive heads could gouge right into the hard disk's surface, ruining your data. If you need to move the computer and hard disk, make sure you "park" the disk drive heads first. A program that parks your PC/IBM compatible computer is available; just install it in your root directory or in your utilities subdirectory if it's in your path—then type "park" and you're set (at least your hard disk is). You can find a program like HARDPARK.EXE from a local Bulletin Board System, or look in a good computer publication for a company that sells public domain and shareware software. This way, either the program is free or you only have to pay for it if you use it and like it.

Some hard disks park themselves automatically when you turn them off. Others won't; you need to run utilities such as the one described above first. Parking the disk drive heads yanks the heads away from the disk. Now you can move the computer and the heads can bounce around all they want—but they'll never come close to scratching the disk.

You don't need to park floppy disk drive heads. Just stick the cardboard packing in your floppy drive, or an old floppy disk, and this gives the floppy drive heads a place to rest if you move the computer.

Hard Disk Optimization

Computers store files on a disk as a continuous strip of information, like a piece of string. As the disk fills up with strips of files, gaps appear in between. The next time you save a file, the computer has to save the file in between the gaps. As you constantly erase or save files, the disk files become fragmented among the different gaps.

The next time the computer needs to find a file, it has to hop, skip, and jump around the disk. Of course this takes time, so you may have to wait awhile until the computer gives you what you want.

To optimize a disk, you need a special disk optimizing program. This program copies all the files off your hard disk and places them back in neat little strips, so that the computer can find them faster next time. There are several good "unfragmenting" programs on the market today that will safely straighten out your hard drive. *Norton Utilities*, *PC-Tools*, and *Mace Utilities*, to name a few, are all good programs that can be purchased for under $100.

Hard Disk Backups

Losing data is a fact of life with computers. Losing hard disk data can push anyone to the point of complete frustration with computers. To prevent catastrophic failures (shades of *The Poseidon Adventure*), buy a hard disk backup program such as *FastBack*.

Hard disk backup programs copy your hard disk files to multiple floppy disks. If your hard disk commits suicide and wipes itself out, just run the hard disk backup program again and the program copies your files from the floppy disks to the hard disk. Of course, you could do this by hand, but hard disk backup programs work faster and more reliably.

CHAPTER 4

Keyboards attract dirt almost as effectively as children. Keeping your keyboard clean is almost as troublesome. You can take your keyboard apart and shake the dirt loose, vacuum out the dirt, or blow the dirt out with a burst of aerosol-propelled air.

These cans of air, sold at photography shops for cleaning cameras, let you blast dust particles right out of the keyboard and into your eyes if you're not careful. If you let dust accumulate in your keyboard, the dust can interfere with the keyboard contacts. If dust sandwiches itself between these contacts, you might type a key and nothing will happen.

Spills, Thrills, and Other Dangers

The biggest danger for keyboards comes from liquid spills. To prevent this problem, keep drinks away from the keyboard. Better yet, if you must drink, store your drinks at a level below the keyboard. That way if you spill anything, it spills on the floor (and all over your shoes) instead of on the keyboard.

Also, you may want to buy a plastic cover for your keyboard. A hard cover protects your keyboard against dust and spills, and also prevents you from typing. Hard covers work only when you aren't using the computer, which means you probably won't be anywhere nearby to spill a drink on the keyboard, either.

Soft covers act like clear membranes for the keyboard. They let you type through them, but they also protect the key board from spills. If you must have your morning coffee, hot chocolate, or cola drink by your side as you type, then a soft keyboard cover can protect your keyboard from those unexpected spills.

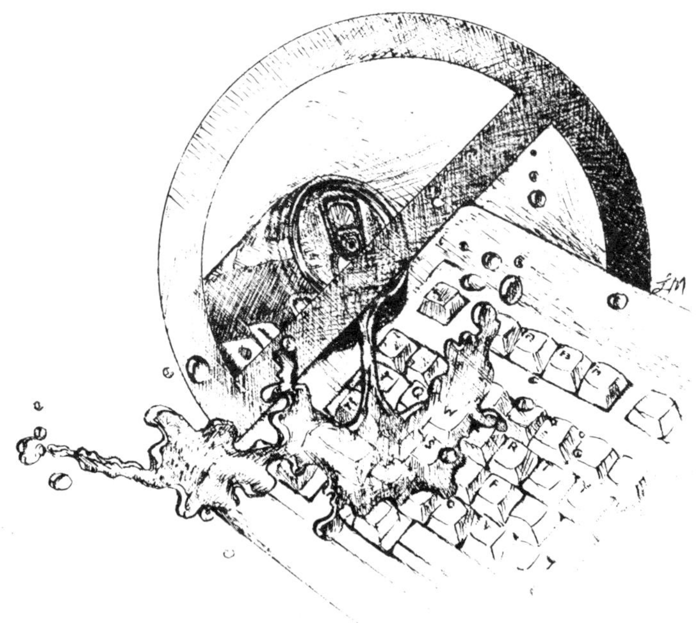

CHAPTER 5

Other Duties

Printers

Dust has to come from somewhere, and the most likely source is your printer. When your printer prints, it tends to rub off flakes of paper and store these flakes as fine white dust inside its case.

You can clean this dust out by blowing real hard and hyperventilating, or you can use a can of compressed air instead. If your vacuum cleaner has a hose, you can clean the dust out of there every week or so.

Paper

As another preventative measure, use quality paper. Cheap paper tends to look and shred like tissue paper, jamming your printer. If you use cheap paper, the printer heads also slam into the platen, which is like banging a fine jeweler's screwdriver tip into the side of a concrete block.

Thicker paper absorbs the blow of the print head, thereby prolonging the print head's life. As another bonus, higher quality paper also won't shred as easily.

When you shop for computer paper, look for 20-pound weight or higher. Also look for laser perforation, which cleanly cuts the paper tractor feed holes away from the main page.

Software

Once your computer works, you need to buy software. After ripping open the software package, find the master disks and write-protect them immediately. Despite the promise of "no copy protection," some programs use a special installation program that counts the number of times you copy the disks. If you try copying the master disk too often, the master disk suddenly copy-protects itself, which is like owning a car that suddenly locks its doors and changes the locks if you're 15 minutes late with your car payment.

Making Backups

After write-protecting your disks, make a backup copy of each one. That way if you should ruin the master disk (the dog eats it or your kid spills marmalade on it), you can still use your backup copy.

As you start creating and saving data, make backup copies of those files, too. Floppy disks multiply like rabbits. One moment you have a nice clean desk with a computer on it, and the next you have several packs of floppy disks scattered across the desk.

Backup disks give you a second chance at life. If you accidentally erase important information, don't scream, curse, or cry. Simply copy your backup disks and you're right back where you started from—which could be right near the beginning if you don't make backup disks regularly.

Taking Care

Caring for your computer takes little time, yet can prevent failure (both your computer's and your career's) in the future should anything go wrong. As a preventative measure, take time once a week to care for the following items, using the checklist below:

The Computer

- Temperature. Is your computer stored in habitable conditions? Remember, direct sunlight can heat up a computer as fast as a blowtorch, so keep your computer away from windows.

- Dust. Can you write your name across the monitor screen?

- Placement. Is the computer secure enough that a minor earthquake won't disturb it?

- Turning it on and off. Do I turn the computer on and leave it unattended for long periods of time? If so, can I turn it on later or turn it off sooner?

Monitor

- Spray glass cleaner. Do I want to turn my $2,000 computer into a personal electric chair? If not, then wait at least one hour before cleaning the monitor with a damp cloth and spray glass cleaner.

- Burn-in. Do I leave the monitor on, displaying the same image for extended periods of time (a couple of hours or so)? If so, then can I get a screen saver program or remember to turn down the monitor each time I leave it?

Disk Drives

- Dust and smoke. Do I store my floppy disks in their protective envelopes and in floppy disk containers? Or do I lay disks around the desk like playing cards, just begging for someone to pick them up and touch their exposed surfaces?

- Types of floppy disks. Do I use the best disks (not necessarily the most expensive disks) possible? Or do my disks keep giving formatting errors?

- Hard disk optimization. Does my hard disk seem slow and make lots of noise when accessing a file? If so, can I use a disk optimization program?

- Hard disk backups. When was the last time I backed up all my valuable files from the hard disk? If it has been longer than a day, then I need a hard disk backup program, 15 minutes, and several boxes of floppy disks in a hurry.

Keyboard

- Spills. Do I keep drinks and food away from the keyboard? If not, do I have a membrane cover for the keyboard?

Printers

- Dust. Do I check the inside of my printer once a week for paper dust buildup? Do I have a can of compressed air or a vacuum cleaner to clean it out?

- Paper. Do I use the best paper I can buy, or am I willing to sacrifice my printer's print heads to save money buying cheap paper more suited for tracing?

Answering these questions regularly can help keep your computer in shape. Take care of your computer and it will take care of you. The two of you can work well together, but only if you make the effort to do so. Happy computing!

PART TWO

REPAIRS
by Scott Millard

CHAPTER 6

Before You Start

What do you do when your hard disk drive stops working or your printer doesn't make those funny noises when your turn it on? It's simple. You figure out what the problems are and then you fix them. You're probably saying to yourself, "There's no way I'm going to take apart this high-tech piece of machinery, I might screw something up." Believe it or not, roughly 90 percent of the problems that occur with computers can be remedied by *you* the owner.

Before we really get into the nitty-gritty of computer repair (it's not that bad, believe me.) I should mention a word of caution. Nothing that this book covers, whether it's the maintenance section or this section, requires a degree in anything, but it is a good idea to be familiar with basic household tools. For example, if you are the kind of person who changes his or her own oil and can fix a flat tire on a car, then this section will be very helpful for you. On the other hand, if you get a little nervous every time you change a light bulb, then I wouldn't suggest trying any of the repairs discussed in this book on your own computer (maybe someone elses' though).

With this in mind, the remaining 10 percent of the problems that your computer can aquire will either be covered by warranty or involve a relatively painless trip to the repair shop. Listed below are some of the problems that you could possibly take on yourself.

Fix it yourself

Hard drive problems—Chapter 8
Floppy drive problems—Chapter 9
Video problems—Chapter 10
Printer problems—Chapter 11
Serial port problems—Chapter 12
Keyboard problems—Chapter 13
Upgrades and changes—Chapter 14
Removing and replacing circuit cards—Chapter 15

If you are mechanically inclined and know how to use standard tools, then many computer problems can be handled in the comfort of your own home. Computers are delicate machines, but basic repairs can be done successfully without any threat to the life of your computer. If you use a pair of pliers and a screwdriver like Rambo uses a machine gun, then maybe computer repair just isn't for you.

CHAPTER 7

Enough forewarning and precautions, it's time to get the prover-bial ball rolling. This chapter will cover the steps you should take before starting any type of computer repair or upgrade job.

Tools

First, you need is the right tools for the job. Luckily there is no need for any special high-zoot tools, as if you were working on an F-14 fighter jet. In fact, you probably already have almost everything you need at home. Here is a list of the tools you will need:

- 1 pair of needle nose pliers
- 1 chip-pulling tool
- 1 small Phillips head screwdriver
- 1 medium-size Phillips head screwdriver
- 1 small flat-blade screwdriver

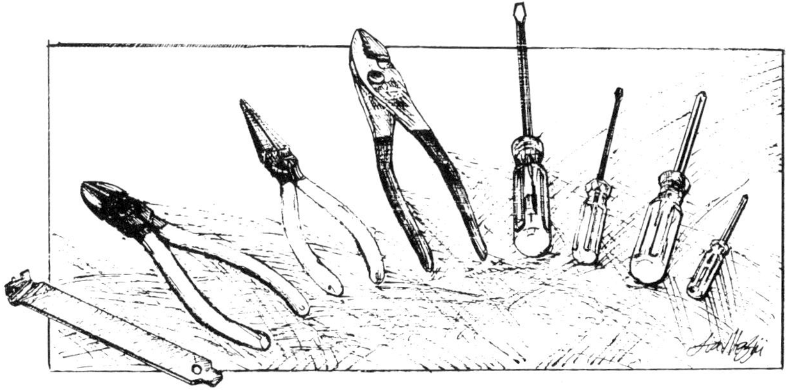

These are the tools that you should make a point to have. If you have more—maybe some regular pliers and another flat-blade screwdriver, then you have nothing to worry about. The one thing that may look foreign to you is the chip-pulling tool. These can be purchased at most computer retail stores and are fairly inexpensive. The funny-looking thing in the preceding illustration is actually an expansion slot cover from a standard PC clone. When used with caution this is an adequate tool for pulling chips.

The Case

Before you do any type of repair or upgrade to your computer, it will most likely require the removal of the computer's case or shell. It doesn't matter if you have a real IBM, a name-brand compatible, or a no-name clone because they all have the same basic design when it comes to their components and how they are put together.

Unplug Everything

Before starting any type of dismantling you have to unplug everything from the wall. After you have done this you should disconnect all of the peripheral devices, such as your printer, monitor, modem, mouse, keyboard, etc., from the back of your computer.

Lift the monitor off your computer (if that's where you had it) and what remains is the computer's CPU or main unit. Usually there are two screws in each side of the computer's case and between three six in the back. This is where your medium-sized Phillips screwdriver will be used. Remove these screws, and the cover should be ready to be lifted off. NOTE: The power supply's fan screws can easily be mistaken for the cover's screws, which are usually in the corners and in the middle. Just remember that not all of the screws on the back hold the cover in place.

If the cover doesn't slide off easily, then there is either a screw yet to be removed, or possibly a cable from the inside snagging something. After carefully checking everything, the cover should come right off.

Identifying the Parts

Once you have the cover removed you will see the brains of your computer exposed for their potential doom. Now it is time to be careful not to drop any foreign objects into your computer—that's right, not even that cigarette you're not supposed to be smoking.

The big boxy looking thing in one corner of your computer's chassis is probably the power supply. This is what provides all of the voltage (very low on the output side) to all of your computer's internal components. You'll notice that the noisy fan you get sick of hearing while trying to talk on the phone is actually part of the power supply. More on this later ...

Toward the front of your computer's chassis are your disk drives. If you have a hard disk drive in addition to a floppy disk drive, the hard disk is probably underneath. Depending on your system, you may or may not have a circuit card (board) hooked to your floppy drive. Some computers, Epsons and Leading Edges for example, have floppy drive controllers built right into the motherboard. Otherwise, there will be a controller card plugged into an expansion slot with a cable running to the drive itself.

The other cards plugged into your motherboard can be for any number of things. If the card takes up the full length of your computer, then it is called a full-length card. I guess you'll know what a half-length card is when you see it. Most device controllers and circuit boards are available in the smaller half-length form, so that computers with smaller footprints (these take up less desk space) will accept the cards.

If your computer has a serial port, parallel port, clock/calendar, bus mouse, or any other type of peripheral port, then these devices are what the rest of the cards in your computer control. Sometimes it is hard to identify which card controls which device, so try and remember where your cables were plugged in. The clock/calendar card will never have any kind of port on the back of it. A port (think of it as an outlet or receptacle) is anything on the back of your computer that allows you to plug in a peripheral device like a printer or mouse.

On the bottom of your computer's chassis a bunch of little black things with legs like cockroaches, along with a bunch of decoratively striped things that look like jewelry. These little beauties are what really make your computer tick—the former being memory chips, BIOS chips, and a processor chip, with the latter being little electronic pieces called resistors and diodes. The silicon chips are the pieces that you can replace on your own. We'll get more into this later on.

CHAPTER 8

Hard Disk Problems

It has been my experience that a hard disk is the one computer component that fails most often. Remember what was said in chapter 1 about turning your computer on only once if you're going to use it periodically during the day. One of the reasons for doing this is to give your hard disk a longer life. Since the hard disk consists of spinning platters and access arms, there are a lot of moving parts. This type of mechanical device is very prone to wear and damage. Unless you accidentally drop your computer down the stairs, the reason it will become inoperable will be due to normal wear and tear.

Detecting a Bad Hard Disk

Detecting a bad hard disk isn't normally a difficult task (thanks to the operating system). If there is a problem you will be lucky if you can boot-up your computer and maybe read a directory. In this case the problem may be that your hard disk isn't capable of reading or writing anymore. Most of the time this problem will occur on only part of the disk. This means that you should immediately back up as many files as you can. If you have access to a utility program like *Norton Utilities*, *Mace Utilities*, or *PC-Tools* you can run a disk test program that will check your hard disk for faulty sectors and/or cylinders, and damaged files. In plain terms, a disk utility program can locate bad parts of your disk and tell your computer not to use them anymore. If there happens to be a file in one of these bad areas of the disk, the utility program will attempt to move its data to a safe place on the disk. If you have already tried this type of fix, and your operating system still gives you the same error messages, then you will probably have to reformat your hard disk and see if that does the trick. Don't worry about a thing, you probably have all of your important data backed up, right?

Your Computer Won't Boot

If you have a problem with your hard disk drive and it won't even let you boot-up your computer, then chances are there is a serious problem. Before you get all psyched up about reformatting your hard drive, you should spend a few minutes to try a couple of things. The first thing you should try if your computer won't boot is using your backup copy of the operating system. Slap that copy of your DOS disk in the A drive and hit the three magic buttons (Ctrl-Alt-Delete). After your computer boots, then try accessing the hard disk. If you get a prompt then there is still hope. Now copy the COMMAND.COM file from the floppy in the hard disk's root directory. Maybe for good measure you should also run the SYS.COM program from the floppy disk to copy the hidden system files over to your hard disk. These files already existed on your hard disk, but for some unknown reason it is possible that at least one of these files could become damaged and unusable. By copying your original files (back ups that is) over the old ones, the problem may be taken care of. This procedure doesn't always guarantee success, but it has worked quite a few times for me.

One more thing you should check is the integrity of your hard disk's data cables. The data cables are the flat ones with a bunch of little wires in a flat row. Sometimes the cable may get jarred loose or it may have gotten pinched or cut by something inside the computer. If this cable turns out to be the problem, then replacing it is as easy as typing DEL *.*.

Formatting a Hard Disk

If everything I mentioned above has failed, and you want to take the plunge into the art of hard disk formatting, the following steps should make the endeavor a bit less painful.

Formatting a hard disk usually consists of a three-step process: 1. Low-Level Formatting, 2. Partitioning, and 3. High-Level Formatting. The exact procedure for formatting a hard drive may vary with the brand of drive and controller card, but the following steps apply to most hard disks for IBM XT and AT compatibles:

- First find your DOS floppy backup and insert it into the A drive.

- **Step 1:** Run the DEBUG.COM utility program. A minus sign (-) will appear below the line you just typed in.

  Type G=C800:5, then hit ENTER.
  (If this doesn't start the formating routine, check with your dealer or your hard disk controller instructions for the right command.)

  Now a series of questions will appear on the screen. First the program will ask which drive you want to format. The default is "C" and that is usually the case. Then the program will warn you that if you continue you will destroy all of the data on your hard disk. Since this is what you want to do, you should answer "yes." Next you will be asked the interleave factor that you wish to use. With most 20- and 30-megabyte hard disks you would choose an interleave factor of 3. This basically means that your hard disk will try seeking information up to three times; if the data is still not found it will either look somewhere else or give you an error. Usually the debug routine will suggest a default interleave for the type of controller you have. Actually, it is a ROM chip on your hard disk controller that is programmed to ask you all of these questions about the low-level format. After the interleave question, the program will ask you if you want to dynamically reconfigure the hard disk. Unless you are feeling extremely adventurous and know all of the specifications of your hard disk, you will want to answer a big "NO" to this question. Next, the program will ask you if you want to format bad sectors. The answer to this question is "no" because the operating system needs to know what sections of the disk shouldn't be read or written to.

There may be a few more questions that come up depending on which controller card you have, but the answers to these are usually defaulted to the right choice. After this brief Q&A session the program will begin to perform a low-level format. It only takes a minute or so with a 30-megabyte drive, so don't run out and get a pizza yet.

■ **Step 2:** Partitioning your hard drive is the next step and is relatively painless. Run the FDISK.EXE program from your DOS disk, and again you will be prompted with a few questions. The first question is, which drive do you want to partition. Then it asks if you want your entire drive to be a DOS partition. Usually this is the case, so you would select the default answer. About 30 seconds later you are done with the partition process and are ready for the last step.

■ **Step 3:** The high-level format is the process that takes the most time. I'm sure you are familiar with the FORMAT command. Well, this time you want to actually type FOR-MAT C:/V/S. There may have been a time in your computing life when you accidentally typed FORMAT C:, and your heart started racing like an Indy car screaming down the straight a way. This time you are actually going to go through with it. The /V portion of the command instructs the computer to prompt you for a volume name that is 11 characters or less. The purpose of the volume name is to let you categorize your disk drives. When you have only one hard disk it's not all that important to do this, but when there are

50 floppy disks sitting around on your desk without labels on the outside, then a volume name is another way to identify the disk. The /S portion of the command tells your computer to copy the necessary operating system files to the C drive.

After the format is completed you will notice the familiar COMMAND.COM file in the root directory of your hard disk. Now you can remove the DOS backup disk from the A drive and reboot your computer with the three magic keys (Ctrl-Alt-Delete).

Replacing a Hard Disk

If you have tried the formatting process mentioned above and your hard drive is still causing nightmares, then it is probably time to replace it. Since it is often hard to diagnose whether or not a hard disk controller is bad, I would recommend replacing it at the same time you replace the hard disk. Usually controllers will be a little more advanced as time goes by, so it definitely can't hurt.

Before getting to the actual removal of the hard disk drive and its controller, you should review Chapter 7 "Getting Ready." After you have done this, the steps listed below will help you complete this procedure without a hitch.

■ **Step 1:** If you have any question as to how the cables are plugged into their respective components, you may want to look at them closely and make a label indicating which end of the cable aligns with which end of the component.

Now you are ready to unplug the power and data cables from the back of the hard disk and controller card. There are two data cables on hard disk drives; one is about twice as wide as the other. Usually these "ribbon cables" are keyed on the end that connects to the hard disk itself. There is a little plastic bar in one slot of the cable's connector that aligns with a slot in the disk drive, so reconnecting this end of the cable is fairly simple. The smaller cable has the same type of connectors as the larger cable. The hard disk controller has a set of pins for each cable to connect to. The tricky part is to find the #1 pin on the card itself. There is usually a "1" painted on the circuit board, next to the #1 pin. The red wire on each cable is the #1 pin wire. Line up this red wire with the #1 pin and the cable will be hooked up correctly. The power cable has three separate wires and a white connector. It is this cable that supplies your hard disk with the voltage to spin the platters and move the read/write heads.

■ **Step 2:** Remove the screw fastening the controller card to the chassis with your medium-sized Phillips screwdriver and carefully rock the card forword and backward while lifting gently. That's all there is to removing a circuit card. When it comes time to replace this card, it really doesn't matter which slot on the motherboard it is plugged into.

■ **Step 3:** Removing the hard drive from the computer's chassis is as easy as taking out four small screws. There are two screws on either side of the drive that often require a small Phillips screwdriver to access. After these screws are removed the drive can be slid out of its mounting bracket from the front of the computer.

In order to reinstall a hard disk you can simply follow the above steps in reverse order. One important thing you will want to know, however, is if the new hard disk is formatted. If so, you can be thankful that all you need to do is install your software. If the drive is not formatted, then you will need to follow the steps I have outlined at the beginning of this chapter. Before you cinch the deal with your local retailer on a new hard drive and controller, be sure to ask if the drive is formatted, and if not, what the low-level debug routine is. Odds are that it will be the same as the one mentioned above if not, you will be glad that you asked.

CHAPTER 9

Floppy Disk Problems

It is not nearly as common for a floppy disk drive to require attention as it is a hard disk, but there are times when one will cease to work. Unfortunately, there is nothing that you can really do if a floppy drive does go bad other than replacing it. However, one must look on the bright side; it really isn't that costly to replace.

Detecting A Bad Floppy Drive

Telltale signs of a bad floppy disk drive occur when the drive is unable to read a disk that was formatted in that same drive. There are some cases where you will insert a disk that a friend gave you and all that you get is a read error. One of the reasons this may happen is that the disk may be a different format. For example: If you tried to read a high-density disk with a 1.2 megabyte format on your 360k drive you will definitely get an error. But, if your friend with a 1.2 megabyte drive tried to read your 360k disk in his computer, he should have no problems. The other reason an error might occur is that the disk you are trying to read was written to by a disk drive with the read/write heads slightly out of whack. If it was your disk drive that wrote to this disk last, and now you can't read the same disk, then you know it is your drive that needs attention.

Removing a Floppy Drive

Chances are you will be able to take either your disk drive or your entire computer to the repair shop so that the heads can be realigned. The cost of a new drive, however, is under $100, so it may not be a bad idea to replace the drive so you don't have to worry about the same thing happening again in the near future.

If you have to remove your floppy drive, either for service or for replacement, first read through Chapter 7 "Getting Ready" and then follow the steps listed below to help you get the job done.

- **Step 1:** Before anything is removed or unplugged, it would be a good idea to look carefully at how the data, or "ribbon cable" is plugged into the floppy drive and its controller. As with the hard disk drive, the data cable is usually keyed on the end that plugs into the drive itself. The connector that plugs into the controller is much like that of a hard disk because it has a red wire for the #1 pin. Even knowing these little tips, you may still want to mark which end of the connector aligns with which end of the component. After doing these precautionary things, you can now unplug both the power and data cables from the floppy drive. The power cable is the same as the one for the hard drive; three separate wires with a white plug on the end of them.

- **Step 2:** Remove the four mounting screws. There are two screws on either side of the drive and you will probably want to use either a medium-sized or a small Phillips screwdriver to remove these. Once these have been removed, slowly slide the disk drive out of the computer's chassis.

There should be no resistance when you slide the drive out of the mounting brackets. If the drive doesn't come out easily, make sure that all of the mounting screws are out and then pay careful attention that the mounting brackets aren't catching the drive's components on their way out.

Reinstalling the drive is as simple as back-stepping through the two steps above. The power cable can go in only one way, and the data cable you already know about.

CHAPTER 10

If you are lucky enough to have conquered the science of disk drive removal and replacement, then the rest of the repairs mentioned here will be a walk in the park. If you haven't messed around with disk drives, then what is covered next is still very simple.

Is it the Monitor or the Display Card?

Usually if a monitor decides to die, you will recognize the problem immediately. As long as everything is plugged in and your computer is on when you turn your monitor on, you should at least see a flashing cursor. If all of the above is true and the little green light is illuminated on your monitor, you should soon see some type of readable character on the screen (give it a minute after you turn on your computer). One thing that I have seen over and over again is the contrast and/or brightness being turned down. If these two adjustments have been checked and still nothing appears, then there is definitely a problem with either your monitor or your display card.

If you are lucky enough to have a friend with the same type of monitor as you (monochrome, CGA, EGA, etc.) then try plugging his or her monitor into your computer. If there is still no sign of life on the screen when the computer powers up, then the problem has been traced to the display board. If you can't remember which port your monitor plugged into, the display board will have a nine-pin female connector. You can tell that it is female if it is something that the cable from your monitor will plug into (monitors most always have male cables).

If you don't have access to another monitor you can take your monitor to a retail store, work, or a friend's and try it there. If the monitor works, then you know for sure that your video card must be bad. If you have a computer with a switchable mono-chrome/CGA card, then you might want to check and see if the switch is set on the proper type.

If you find that your monitor doesn't work when plugged into another computer, then I'm afraid the Cathode Ray Tube or some other component inside the monitor might be bad, and a trip to the shop is required.

Removing and Replacing a Display Card.

It will probably take you the same amount of time to read the steps to removing a display card as it will to remove one, but it is important to be careful and to do the right thing. See Chapter 15 for the proper procedures.

CHAPTER 11

Printer Problems

Fixing a printer is not always entirely possible, but there are certain instances when your printer might stop working, and fixing it will take just a few minutes. Then again, there are times when the only thing left to do is take your printer to the repair shop for the pros to look at.

Nothing Will Print

If you have just bought a new printer or you're trying a different printer on your computer, it is not uncommon to get everything hooked up, load your word processor, hit the print command and have nothing come out on the printer. In order to solve this problem there are a few things I suggest you check out:

- **Step 1:** The first thing you want to do is make sure your printer is on-line. You may laugh now, but if that little on-line light isn't lit up, then nothing is ever going to come out of that printer. Since the on-line button works like a toggle switch, you can simply press the on-line button once to make the printer ready to receive data.

- **Step 2:** Make sure that paper is fed into the printer properly and that the "paper out" light is not illuminated. If everything looks OK here, then the printer is as good as ready.

■ **Step 3:** It is not uncommon to plug a printer into the wrong port when it is first hooked up to your computer. If you have a serial printer you would want it hooked up to your serial port. But these days most people buy and sell parallel printers, so you would want to hook your printer to the parallel port. The parallel port is always the 25-pin female port on the back of your computer. If you are not sure that your printer is plugged into the right port, then plug it into the other port that the cable will fit in. If there isn't another port, then chances are you only have a parallel port and the cable was plugged into the right port to begin with.

After trying each one, or all of the above checks, you will want to try printing something to see if you have solved the problem. The easiest way to do this is not to get into a word processor and hit the print command. The easiest way to check your printer is to type DIR at the DOS prompt to get anything on the screen. Then just hit Shift-Print Screen and whatever you have on the screen should be sent to the printer. Another easy way is to hold down the Ctrl key and hit P to toggle the printer on. Now everything that you type at the keyboard will be sent to the printer. If nothing happens, then there is definitely something wrong with either the printer, the cable, the printer card, or possibly the MODE command.

In order to fix the cable problem, you can either buy a new cable or borrow one from a friend. If after trying a different cable your printer still doesn't work, then you know the problem was not in the cable. Another test you can try is to take your printer to another computer and try it there, using the cable that was already hooked up to that computer. If none of these tests work, then chances are it is either the printer itself or the parallel port that is bad.

The next thing to try should be the MODE command in your operating system. The MODE command in MS-DOS actually affects more than just printer output. With this command you are able to control printer characteristics, display characteristics, and serial port characteristics. If you have a serial printer and you need to check the serial port on your computer, refer to Chapter 12 under the section "Determining What The Problem Is".

For parallel printers (specifically all Epson, Epson compatible, and IBM matrix and graphics printers) the MODE command should look like this: MODE LPT1

This will assure you that anything that you are trying to print on your computer will be sent through the #1 parallel port.

If after trying all of these things you still can't get anything to print, you will probably need a new parallel or serial port.

The final test would be to hook someone else's printer up to your computer and give the old Print Screen command a try. If the printer then starts to make its loud printing noises, you know for sure that your printer is bad. On the other hand, if your printer and cable work on another computer and the mode command had been typed in correctly on your computer, then you probably have a bad port on your computer. To install a new port, refer to Chapter 15 "Removing And Replacing Miscellaneous Circuit Cards."

If it Stops Printing

There are a number of things that can go wrong with a printer that may cause it to suddenly stop printing. If the cause is a bad cable you can follow the suggested steps above to pinpoint that as the problem. If the problem is internal to the printer, I would recommend checking the printer's ribbon. If the print head suddenly stops moving while in the middle of a 20-page report due in one hour, you don't want the problem to be electrical. If you're lucky, like I have been in the past, the culprit here was the case of a jammed-up ribbon cartridge causing the print head to stop. If this happens to you, all you need to do is pop the ribbon cartridge off and try turning the advancement knob on the cartridge with your fingers. If you feel a lot of resistance, then this is most likely what caused the problem. Sometimes just twisting this little knob a bit will do the trick. You can either try to free the stuck ribbon or go to your computer supply drawer and open up a new ribbon. You do have at least one extra ribbon lying around, don't you?

I have tried taking apart a ribbon cartridge and it's not a pretty sight. Unless you have a few pairs of surgical gloves and a lot of patience, you probably won't want to mess with your old printer ribbon.

It Won't Turn On

Another problem you may have with your printer is that it will not initialize when you turn it on. If you're lucky the problem will be hiding in a bad connection in your parallel cable. Check and see if your plugs are solidly seated and that the contacts are clean. If that doesn't work, make sure the cable ends are not pulling out of the connectors. Wiggling the ends of the cable while you are trying to print or after you have turned on your printer sometimes will tell you if there is a bad connection. If this is the case, you will most likely have to replace the cable.

If the cable is not the problem, then I'm afraid the only thing left is either the printer or the port that is driving the printer. The way to test either of the two components is to try either another printer, or take your printer to your friend's house, or even a dealer, and see if it works there. If it turns out that you do have to replace the parallel port, then refer to Chapter 15.

CHAPTER 12

Serial Port Problems

You may not be very happy if you just spent over $100 on a brand- new serial mouse or an external modem and you find out that the thing doesn't work. Well, before you take the product back to Joe's Computer Store or throw it through the window, make sure that you have a functional serial port. I have seen it happen before. A friend of mine bought a new serial mouse, hooked it up, and he soon found that the little pointing device didn't do a darn thing. As it turns out the problem was in the serial port, and the reason it was never discovered before is that this was the first time Ed tried to use it. After trying all of the different COM# settings with the DOS MODE command, checking switches, and running test programs supplied with the mouse, we determined that the problem had to be with the serial port. After buying a new serial port and plugging it in (see Chapter 15) everything was hunky-dory. NOTE: Two serial ports with the same memory addresses will not run at the same time. Therefore, you will have to be certain the old serial port is either disconnected, set to a different COM#, or removed altogether from your computer before you put in a new one.

Determining What the Problem Is

There are times when an inoperable mouse may be the fault of the mouse or the lack of the appropriate software, but this is a sure way to check your serial port. If you were to have the same experience as Ed, except with an external modem, there are ways of checking your serial port also. In the better modem manuals and a book published by CPE entitled "How to Get Started with Modems" there are examples of ways to test both the modem and the serial port for error-free operation. The basic gist of it is that a series of basic Hayes commands can be used to send data through the serial port to the modem.

One thing that you should definitely try when you have a serial device that won't work is the MODE command, as I mentioned above. If you are trying to make sure your serial port is being recognized by the operating system, the following commands will help:

When using a serial port with a printer, type:

MODE LPT1: = COM1

This tells your operating system that everything that is normally sent out the parallel port will now be sent out the serial port. (i.e. Ctrl P, and Print Screen)

For using a modem, serial mouse, or another serial device, type the following:

MODE COM1:2400 (or) MODE COM2:2400

Either one of these commands will tell your operating system which COM port to send data out of when a serial device is being used. The 2400 following the colon tells the operating system what baud rate the port should use. This number could be any of the nine settings a serial port will accept.

One COM port is distinguished from another by its hardware setting. In other words, if you have a serial mouse and your serial port is set for COM1, then an internal modem would have to be set for COM2. The MODE command would then be used with COM2 for directing serial output through the modem.

If any type of problem occurs with your serial port, whether it be a mouse, modem, or printer, it is a good idea to test the port before running over your new mouse with your car. If it turns out that it is the port that is bad, then you should simply replace it as described in Chapter 15.

CHAPTER 13

Keyboard Problems

Keyboards have got to be the easiest things to replace on a desktop computer, next to inserting and removing floppy disks. Typically, when a keyboard goes bad it becomes difficult to type certain keys. It is possible that all you need to do is take your keyboard apart and clean it out. To clean out a keyboard follow these steps:

- **Step 1:** Remove the screws on the back of the keyboard. There will be between two and six screws that you will have to remove.

- **Step 2:** Release any levers or tabs that need releasing and gently separate the two halves of the keyboard.

- **Step 3:** Slowly and carefully remove each key. The keys are usually snapped into place, but be sure to remember where they all go.

- **Step 4:** Use a soft cloth to wipe clean the open surfaces under the key posts. To clean the contacts themselves you may want to use a Q-tip and a little rubbing alcohol, or a soft cloth with a toothpick and rubbing alcohol. Each key actually has its own little switch with some sort of metal for contact.

- **Step 5:** Reassemble all of the parts in the reverse order.

If your keyboard continues to behave poorly or if it just doesn't work at all, it is time for a new one. In this case, buy a new one and plug it in.

CHAPTER 14

Upgrades and Changes

Upgrading microprocessors is probably more common than having to replace a microprocessor for being faulty. However, if your computer gets past the RAM test when you boot it up and then suddenly stops or gets an error, it could be a bad processor chip. You can buy a new microprocessor for XT compatibles for about $20 so it is actually a good opportunity to upgrade your machine if you have a slower turbo or even a single-speed chip at present. If you don't feel like going through the trial and error method of repair, then you might want to take your computer to a dealer for repairs.

Processor Chips

Whether you want to change your processor or add a math co-processor, you will perform the same steps. In order to remove and replace a processor chip you need to do the following:

- **Step 1:** Locate the processor chip on your motherboard. If you know what kind of processor you have, then look for one of the bigger chips on the board that is sitting next to an empty socket. This empty socket is where a math co-processor would go if you wish to install one. The chip should have its manufacturer's name and its model number stamped right on the top. For example, an Intel 8088-2 chip will have this information on the top of the chip.

- ■ **Step 2:** Use either a chip-removing tool or a spare expansion slot cover as shown in Figure 3 to remove the processor chip. Carefully pry each end of the chip up about a sixteenth of an inch at a time. After the chip feels loose, grab the chip with your fingers and gently lift it straight out of the socket.

- ■ **Step 3:** When you replace the chip be sure that the notch in one end of the chip matches the notch in the socket. Tilt the chip slightly to one side and slowly slip those legs into the socket, making sure that each leg sits in a hole. After one side of legs is positioned, tilt the chip the other direction to seat the legs on the other side. After all of the legs are lined up, carefully push straight down on the chip to seat the legs fully.

Now you have effectively performed a brain transplant in your very own computer. If you have chosen a faster chip, whether for upgrade reasons or repair reasons I'm sure you will notice a difference in speed.

ROM Chip

ROM chips aren't any easier to diagnose as faulty than a processor chip, but they are just as easy to replace. To locate your ROM chip on your motherboard, it also helps to know who the manufacturer is. For example, if you have a Phoenix BIOS, then your ROM chips will have the name Phoenix stamped on them. Usually ROM chips come in pairs, so the chips to look for are the larger chips (about the same size as a processor chip) that are sitting side by side.

If you have continuous problems with crashing or you get a lot of input/output errors, then chances are it is your ROM chip(s) that is bad. To replace or upgrade your ROM BIOS chips, refer to the steps above for replacing a microprocessor chip.

CHAPTER 15

Removing and Replacing Miscellaneous Circuit Cards

For the purpose of this book the category of miscellaneous circuit cards is made up of parallel ports, serial ports, clock/calendars, game ports, multi-function boards, bus mouses, display cards, and internal modems. When you are dealing with IBM PC and compatible machines, it really doesn't matter what type of circuit card you are removing and replacing; the process is identical for all.

Before starting on any one of these delicate little jewels, make sure that you have followed all of the steps in Chapter 7 "Getting Ready." After this it's as simple as 1-2-3 (NO, not Lotus).

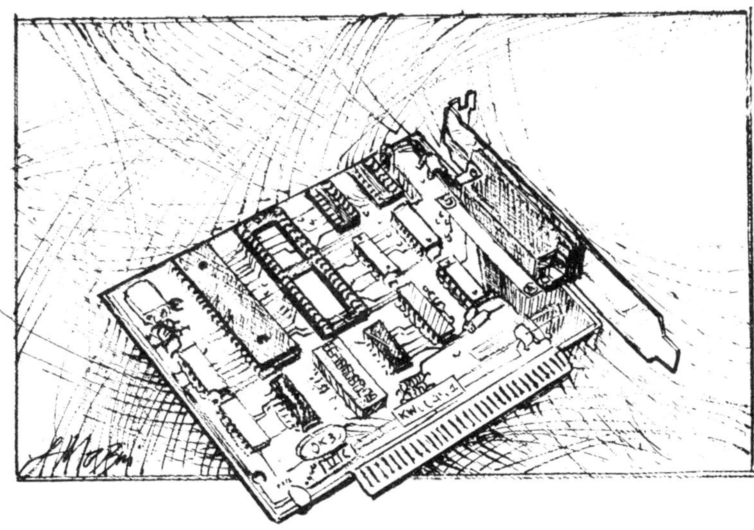

- Step 1: Remove the screw fastening the card to the computer's chassis with a medium-sized Phillips screwdriver.

- Step 2: Gently grasp the card and rock it forward and backward while carefully lifting up. The card should come out without much effort.

- Step 3: To reinstall the card, just perform the above two steps in reverse order. It doesn't matter which expansion slot you choose when you plug the card back into the computer. You may want to think about which ones you will want available for later expansion. If you have an AT 286 or 386 computer, there will be both 16-bit and eight-bit expansion slots. Eight-bit expansion cards will work in 16-bit slots, but you should try and save the bigger slots for cards that require them.

If you are installing any type of expansion board, refer to the instructions provided with that board to determine what DIP switch or jumper settings should be set. These switches will change the operation of the board according to the function you want it to perform or the type of computer you are installing it in. There is usually a pretty good description of what to do with these switches in most installation guides.

CHAPTER 16

Putting It All Back Together

Keep in mind that for all the tasks mentioned above, you first have to have the cover off of your computer as I discussed in the beginning of this section. Of course, this also means that when you are finished with these same tasks, that the cover has to be put back on so the cat won't jump on your motherboard thinking it's her new bed.

Replacing the computer cover is obviously not difficult, especially if you have already successfully completed any of the above tasks. One thing that you do want to watch for is that all of the cables and wires are tucked safely out of harm's way. Be sure that there aren't any cables too close to the power supply and that nothing is sticking up high enough to get caught on the cover when you slide it back on. Double-check all of the connections and brackets to make sure they are snug and secure. It really isn't necessary to get any of the screws ultra-tight on a computer because you're not driving it around every day like a car or truck.

Now I suppose it is time to slip the cover carefully on. As with its removal, the cover should not have to be forced on at all. The holes should all line up and everything should fit through their respective slots. Replace the screws that hold the cover in place and snug them up with your Phillips screwdriver.

Plugging It All Together

Since you have seen the inside of your computer, you now have a better idea of what all of the ports on the back connect to and what they do. The only two ports that you may get confused are the serial and parallel ports, but if you plug your printer into one and it doesn't work, just plug it into the other port and I'll bet that you have found your parallel port.

After hooking up your monitor and keyboard, it is time to fire up the old electronic brain. I can't guarantee it, but I'll bet that your pet computer will work as good as new.

One Last Word Of Caution

Unfortunately, I can't promise that everything I have gone through in this section will solve all of the computer problems you will ever have, but I can say that everything discussed here I have done myself with great success. Just remember that being careful and keeping things like magnets, big heavy tools, and hot things away from your computer while working on it is the best caution you can exercise.

Don't forget that maintaining your computer system as discussed in the first section is the best thing you can do to prevent any possible problems down the road. Hopefully, if you do encounter problems, your warranty will still be in effect, and if not, then you now know how to perform a majority of the needed repair work yourself.

INDEX

M

miscellaneous circuit cards
 bus mouses, 51
 clock callendars, 51
 display cards, 51
 game ports, 51
 internal modems, 51
 multi-function, 51
 parallel ports, 51
 serial ports, 51
MODE.COM, 42, 45
monitor tips, 7, 8
 burn-in, 7
 cleaning, 7

P

paper, 15
perventative maintence
 hot temperatures, 4
plugging it together, 54
ports, 26
power on and off, 4
power supply, 24
power surges, 5
preventative maintenance, 3
 burn-in period, 4
 cold temperatures, 4
 on and off, 4
 power surges, 5
 storage, 6
printer problems, 41, 42, 43, 44
 MODE.COM, 42
 nothing prints, 41
 ribbon cartridge, 44
printers, 15
 paper, 15
processor chips, 49
 Intel 8088-2, 49
putting it together, 53, 54

R

RAM test, 49
removing a floppy drive, 36
replacing a hard disk, 31
ribbon cartridge, 44
ROM chips, 50
 Phoenix BIOS, 50
root directory, 28

S

serial port problems, 45, 46
 COMn settings, 45
 determining the problem, 45
smoke, 9
software, 16
storing your computer, 6
SYS.COM, 28

T

tools, 23

U

upgrades & changes, 49, 50
 processor chips, 49
 ROM chips, 50

V

video problems, 39, 40
 display card, 39

W

word of caution, 54

Other computer books from
Computer Publishing Enterprises:

How to Understand and Buy Computers
by Dan Gookin

How to Understand and Find Software
by Wally Wang

Parent's Guide to Educational Software and Computers
by Lynn Stewart and Toni Michael

How to Get Started With Modems
by Jim Kimble

How to Start a Business With a Computer
by Jack Dunning

Ten (& More) Interesting Uses for Your Home Computer
by Tina Berke

101 Computer Business Ideas
by Wally Wang

The Best FREE Time-Saving Utilities for the PC
by Wally Wang